Geography

New York

By Sarah De Capua

Consultant
Nanci Vargus, Ed.D.
Primary Multiage Teacher
Decatur Township Schools, Indianapolis, Indiana

New Yor   ydney
Me
Danbury, Connecticut

Designer: Herman Adler Design
Photo Researcher: Caroline Anderson
The photo on the cover shows the Adirondack State Park in New York.

Library of Congress Cataloging-in-Publication Data

De Capua, Sarah.
  New York / by Sarah De Capua.
    p. cm. — (Rookie read-about geography)
Includes index.
Summary: Introduces the state of New York and its cities and towns,
geographical features, interesting sights, and more.
  ISBN 0-516-22665-7 (lib. bdg.)   0-516-27490-2 (pbk.)
  1. New York (State)—Juvenile literature. 2. New York (State)—
Geography—Juvenile literature. [1. New York (State)] I. Title. II. Series.
  F119.3 .D4 2002
  917.47—dc21
                                  2002005502

CHILDREN'S PRESS, AND ROOKIE READ-ABOUT®,
and associated logos are trademarks and or registered trademarks
of Grolier Publishing Co., Inc. SCHOLASTIC and associated logos
are trademarks and or registered trademarks of Scholastic Inc.
1 2 3 4 5 6 7 8 9 10 R 11 10 09 08 07 06 05 04 03 02

Do you know where you can find the Adirondack Mountains?

They are in the state of
New York! Can you find
New York on this map?
It is in the northeastern
United States.

CANADA

WASHINGTON

OREGON

IDAHO

MONTANA

NORTH
DAKOTA

MINNESOTA

WYOMING

SOUTH
DAKOTA

WISCONSIN

MICHIGAN

NEW HAMPSHIRE

VERMONT

MAINE

NEW YORK

MASSACHUSETTS

RHODE ISLAND

CONNECTICUT

NEVADA

UTAH

COLORADO

NEBRASKA

IOWA

ILLINOIS

INDIANA

OHIO

PENNSYLVANIA

NEW JERSEY

DELAWARE

WEST
VIRGINIA

MARYLAND

CALIFORNIA

KANSAS

MISSOURI

KENTUCKY

VIRGINIA

Washington, D.C.

ARIZONA

NEW MEXICO

OKLAHOMA

ARKANSAS

TENNESSEE

NORTH
CAROLINA

ALABAMA

GEORGIA

SOUTH
CAROLINA

TEXAS

MISSISSIPPI

LOUISIANA

FLORIDA

North

West

East

South

ALASKA

CANADA

MEXICO

HAWAII

5

Long Island is part of New York. Many beaches are found on the island's shore.

The Adirondack and Catskill Mountains cover much of New York. Mount Marcy is in the Adirondack Mountains. It is the highest point in the state.

New York's forests are full
of pine, spruce, sugar maple,
and birch trees.

The sugar maple is New York's state tree.

Most of New York's farmland is found in the northern and western areas of the state. Farmers raise cows and grow apples, corn, hay, and vegetables.

There are thousands of lakes in New York.

The Finger Lakes are some of the best-known lakes in the state.

New York City is the
largest city in New York.
About eight million people
live there.

One of its famous landmarks is the Empire State Building.

Albany is New York's capital city. It is located on the Hudson River. Other important cities include Buffalo, Rochester, and Syracuse.

Albany

20

In the cities, most people work in factories or office buildings. The factories make clothing and electronics.

New York has small towns too. Red House is the smallest town in the state. Only 38 people live there. Many of the people who live in New York's small towns work as farmers or miners.

24

New York is snowy in
the winter and warm in
the summer.

Animals such as black
bears, coyotes, foxes,
beavers, and porcupines
are found in New York.

Many kinds of birds, including wild turkeys, robins, and sparrows are found in New York. The bluebird is the state bird of New York.

Some people like New York because of its busy, crowded cities.

Others like the quiet places
in nature. What is your
favorite place in New York?

Words You Know

bluebird

Empire State Building

farmland

forest

Long Island

mountains

New York City

sugar maple

31

Index

About the Author

Sarah De Capua is an author and editor of children's books. She resides in Colorado. The author wishes to thank Edward Knoblauch and Rachel Rubin of The Encyclopedia of New York State for their gracious assistance.

Photo Credits

Photographs © 2002: Envision/Henryk T. Kaiser: 10, 30 bottom right; Peter Arnold Inc./Robert Mackinlay: cover; Photo Researchers, NY/Rafael Macia: 7, 31 top left; Superstock, Inc.: 14, 28; The Image Works: 21 (David Lassman), 29 (Daniel Wray); Tom Till: 3, 8, 11, 31 bottom right, 31 top right; Visuals Unlimited: 25, 26 (Bill Banascewski), 19, 24 (Steve Callahan), 27, 30 top left (Gary W. Carter), 16, 17, 30 top right, 31 bottom left (Jeff Greenberg), 20 (D. Long), 12, 23, 30 bottom left (L.S. Stepanowicz), 13 (E. Webber).

Maps by Bob Italiano